FIRST AID
AND NURSING
FOR
WILD
BIRDS

FIRST AID
AND NURSING
FOR
WILD
BIRDS

DOREEN KING

Whittet Books

TITLE PAGE ILLUSTRATION: hand-rearing wild birds can be very satisfying and rewarding.

First published 1994
© 1994 by Doreen King
Whittet Books Ltd, 18 Anley Road, London W14 OBY

British Library Cataloguing in Publication Data
A catalogue record for this book is available from the British Library
ISBN 1 873580 15 0

Printed and bound in Great Britain by
Biddles Ltd, Guildford and King's Lynn

(Intervet)

ACKNOWLEDGMENT

The author would like to thank the London Borough of Havering for an Arts Bursary Scheme award towards the cost of information technology equipment. The author would also like to thank Intervet UK Ltd for their generous support.

CONTENTS

1 FIRST CONSIDERATIONS

So you found an injured or sick wild bird and took it home. Now you must decide what to do with it.

BABY BIRDS

Thousands of baby birds are picked up and taken home every year by children, who think that they have been abandoned. Birds do not, in general, abandon their young. However, baby birds may crash land on their maiden flights and be in considerable danger from cats. If you have found a feathered, apparently healthy young bird, such as a sparrow, which will have a bright yellow rim around its beak (an aid to the parent birds when feeding it), then do see if it can possibly be taken back to where it was found and left in a hiding place where cats cannot reach it. Watch at a distance, or return an hour later to see if it is being fed.

This is easier said than done. Young birds are very vulnerable and in towns and cities they are found on roads and in markets and all manner of unusual places. Furthermore, if there are no trees nearby and you put, for instance, a sparrow on an exposed wall, a cat or a crow will surely take it. Also, birds

Two days after arrival, and after bathing its eyes four times, the blue tit's eyes were fully open.

such as blue tits take their new families on journeys of considerable distance in search of food, and after about an hour or two, a young blue tit is most unlikely to be able to attract its parents because they will have moved away. So, if this option is not feasible, you may have to bring the young bird up yourself.

Sometimes, young birds are thrown out of the nest by the parents or by their brothers and sisters. This often happens to weak birds and those that have something wrong with them such as abnormal colouring or blindness. Young cuckoos will throw out all the legitimate siblings in a nest. It would obviously be unwise to replace such birds as they will be thrown out again and if you disturb the nest the parents may desert. Escapees are often found as a result of attacks by crows and cats. Young birds will also try to leave the nest if the parents have died or deserted them. Siblings of young birds of prey will sometimes eat the one that is last to hatch but occasionally such birds will be found, having 'escaped' from the nest. Owls may leave the nest before they can fly properly, and they should be left alone if they are in a secure location. Check to see that they are all right an hour or so later. Certain birds are protected, and it is a legal requirement that you consult the Department of the Environment before approaching the nest (see p.94).

If you find a downy pigeon it should be in a nest, and it will need to be hand-reared.

Young feathered herons, like pigeons, often fall from their nests; since they are only fed at the nest, they will starve unless they can be hand-reared.

If a whole nest has fallen down and the youngsters are feathered, then it would be extremely difficult to attempt to put the nest back as the birds will probably try to leave it. Do not attempt to put a feathered bird back into a nest; nesting birds should not be disturbed and the process may upset the rest of

8

the brood. You will now have to hand-rear the bird — or find someone else to do so.

Adult Birds

It is unnatural for an adult bird (or a bird that has been out of the nest for more than a day or so) to allow a person to pick it up. If you can, then you must assume that there is something drastically wrong with it.

Primary Care

The best thing to keep a bird in is a cardboard box, into which you make some small holes for ventilation. Line the box with newspaper and put the bird in; if it is unfeathered, wrap it in old material; socks, woolly hats, or tissues are good. Put the box on a warm hot-water bottle, heating pad or radiator. Sometimes merely resting the bird in the box for half an hour will enable the bird to recover.

Remember that a baby bird should not be left for more than a couple of hours without being fed.

Before deciding what to do with it, wash your hands. Birds carry diseases. *Always wash your hands after touching them.* Birds should be treated as soon as possible, so you should decide whether you will try to look after the bird yourself, and whether it should go to the vet. You have a legal right to nurse a wild bird casualty, but it is illegal to keep a rare wild bird without a licence. Lists of such birds are available from the Department of the Environment and getting a licence is simply a matter of registering the bird and paying a fee. It is a legal requirement to ring certain types of rare bird if kept in permanent captivity, but exemption can be obtained if the bird's disability would make ringing impractical. The Department of the Environment will supply a suitable ring.

The bird can be examined easily as it is held loosely. However, care is needed as the wings should never be allowed to flap.

The law is there to protect the rehabilitator and the bird, and to prevent the trade in capturing wild birds and selling them for profit, especially in the case of falcons, which are in demand for falconry.

A bird licence is like any other licence: it normally lasts three years. Licensing is just a registration process and does not mean that the licence holder is any better at keeping birds than anyone else. Persons who have obtained a suitable number of licences (three per year for three consecutive years) can apply for a special rehabilitation licence (Licensed Rehabilitation Keeper) which will reduce the cost. It only applies to keeping birds for up to six weeks and it is stressed that such a licence does not give the right to mistreat any bird.

Your local vet should be able to give you the name of a local contact who can take the bird or offer you advice if you wish to nurse it yourself. Unfortunately there is a great need for more people to act as local contacts. You might find a contact in the telephone directory. Remember that if you decide to nurse it, you will probably need to keep it for at least two to six weeks, and remember too that birds sometimes need to be force fed. Feathered baby birds must be fed from dawn until about 10 p.m., and unfeathered birds and new arrivals will generally need feeding during the night as well.

It is obviously advisable to ask your vet to look at the bird, especially if it is badly injured or looks as though it is diseased. If you do take the bird to a vet, do explain that if the bird does stand some chance of recovery, then you or your contact (if you have found someone else who will take over the care of the bird) are willing to nurse it. Otherwise, the vet may think that you want it destroyed. For the same reason never leave a bird at the surgery. If the bird has badly damaged wings then you, or your contact, must decide whether it can be offered a reasonable life in permanent captivity, should it recover.

RINGED BIRDS

The treatment of racing pigeons is covered in Chapter 2. The owners of show birds can usually be traced. If you found a bird with the letters BC, contact the British Bird Council, and for rings with the letters IoA, contact the International Ornithological Associaton. For falcons, contact the Department of the Environment. In general, the owners of injured show birds will not want them back.

If a wild bird has been found with a British Trust for Ornithology ring, then do inform them about what happened to the bird, especially if it died. Give them the ring number, date and place where it was found, and the circumstances.

2 TREATMENT

Before you decide on what treatment is appropriate for the bird, examine it thoroughly. Do not hold it too tightly, or allow the wings to flap. It is sometimes easier to wrap a bird in a cloth (see the section on handling, p. 80).

Quick guide to action

baby birds	feed immediately
broken bones	the bones will need to be strapped into place
cuts	disinfect, and your vet will be able to give it an antibiotic
listless birds	check for injuries and disease and offer food
signs of disease and infection	identify signs of disease and consult your vet

Keep a record of the bird — when it arrived, what had happened to it, and details of its treatment and release.

If a bird needs any form of treatment, keep it warm, preferably at 28° C (refer to section on housing, p. 73). It would be wise to keep all newly arrived birds isolated for the first couple of days.

With injuries, there is always the possibility of damage to organs and internal haemorrhaging leading to sudden death. Birds that have lost a lot of blood will be anaemic; in these

This blue tit was probably ejected from the nest because it had not opened its eyes.

cases, warmth, rest and plenty of food and water is necessary. Give ½ teaspoon of vitamin supplement (for example, SA37, see p. 93) daily for about seven days. Whilst the birds are undergoing treatment, feed them on easily digestible foods; for instance, change the diet of pigeons to small seeds and avoid greens.

Your vet will usually be able to discuss with you any proposed treatment and nursing. Any potentially painful procedures should be carried out by your vet. The more intelligent birds are likely to remember if someone hurts them and this will make any subsequent nursing difficult if it is carried out by the same person. Conditions such as prolapse can be treated by a vet. However, prolapse may recur and in some cases your vet may advise euthanasia.

Homoeopathy

The word homoeopathy means the treatment of disease by using small amounts of a drug that, in healthy persons, produces symptoms similar to those being treated.

It is always best to consider all treatments available and to follow treatments that are known to be successful first. In any event, the course of treatment used should always be discussed fully with a vet.

Homoeopathic preparations that have been used with some success on birds include:

aconite	for shock
silicea	for pellet wounds (use for one day only)
calendula	for open wounds
carbo-vegitabilis	for the revival of 'almost dead' birds
arnica	for traumatized birds
hypericum	for pain relief after surgery. On no account should this be used instead of an anaesthetic or prescribed analgesics
hepar-sulph	for the healing of abscesses
calcarea phosphorica	for the healing of broken bones

carbo-vegitablilis and *arnica* are particularly useful for birds

The usual dose of homoeopathic substances for birds is one tablet of 200 strength daily. It can be given in one dose or as two ½ tablets with a one-hour interval in between. The tablets can be crushed and added to food. Creams and ointments are usually applied generously.

ALPHABETICAL GUIDE TO COMMON AILMENTS

Air sacs

Bird casualties sometimes have swellings under the skin that are filled with air. They look like bubbles, and are soft to the touch. Bird skin is very fine and you will see that the sacs are filled with air. These usually result from trauma and therefore may be indicative of more serious internal injuries. In the rare event that the air sac is at the side of the neck, the bird may be unable to eat; then the air sac may be pierced by a sterile needle; a vet will be able to do this for you. If the air sac recurs, then gas-forming bacteria should be suspected and your vet will usually give an antibiotic. Air sacs may also prevent flying. But usually they clear up after a couple of weeks.

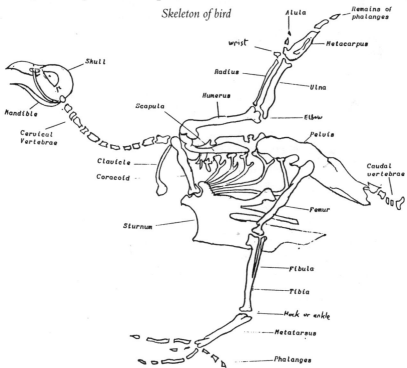

Skeleton of bird

15

Broken beak

A broken beak can be extremely distressing for a bird. Simple fractures may heal. For small breaks you can use surgical tape (micropore tape is suitable) for two to four weeks, depending on the size of the bird's beak. The tape can be reinforced with a sliver of plastic but the tape can only cover the top or bottom of the beak. Do not put tape all around the beak, and if the break is on the top half of the beak, you must avoid covering the nostrils. It is always best to consult a vet. If the tip of the beak has broken off this may grow back again.

Broken bones

Broken bones should be treated as soon as possible. Even after only one day, the bone may begin to heal and it may then be difficult to set it properly. You should seek veterinary assistance about broken bones, especially in the case of large birds, and in the case of compound fractures where the bones are protruding. Examine the bird for broken bones carefully. Run your fingers along the bones and feel for any displacement and/or abnormal movement. Compare the injured limb to the normal one. Do not keep a limb immobilized in a splint for longer than necessary, as ankylosis (stiffening) and arthritis may set in. Ten days should be long enough for simple breaks in small birds. Micropore tape or zinc oxide plaster is suitable for strapping broken bones. Remember that it may be a week or two after the splint is removed before the bird becomes fully mobile again, especially in the case of large birds.

Broken legs

If the skin is broken, disinfect, as explained under cuts and bites (see p. 24).

Immobilize the bird by wrapping it in a cloth and run your fingers along its leg. You may then be able to feel the break

(ABOVE) Carefully position the splint over the break.
(BELOW) The splint can be trimmed once it is in place.

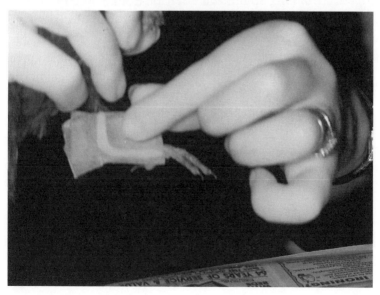

17

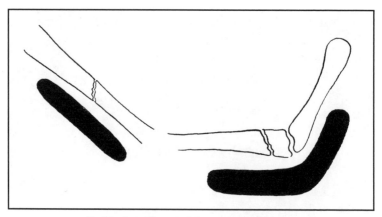

Positioning splints on joints and straight bones.

and the unnatural movement associated with the break. If the break is in between two joints the splint can be placed in between the two joints. If the break involves a joint, then part of the leg before and after the joint will need to be included in the splint.

For small birds splints can be made from plastic food containers such as margarine tubs. Cut out a strip of plastic and trim it to the desired size. The plastic strip can be wrapped in sticky plaster to add a little padding. The splint is positioned on one piece of surgical tape to which it will adhere (micropore tape is suitable). Add the splint to one side of the leg and then add another piece of tape to the other side of the leg. The ends of the tape are pressed together to enclose the limb and then the ends can be trimmed as necessary. If additional support is necessary a splint can be placed on each side of the leg.

For larger birds, matchsticks or lolly sticks may be used.

Keep the splint in place for about ten days for minor breaks in small birds. For very severe breaks in large birds it may be necessary to keep the splint in place for up to four weeks.

Birds may limp for a number of reasons. Seabirds that are out of water for a while may limp due to drying out of their delicate feet. Apply cod-liver oil or cooking oil if this is the case. Birds may also limp due to infection of the 'knee' (see diseases, p. 46).

Many species of bird can manage quite well with only one leg, and very badly damaged legs can be amputated by a vet as a last resort.

Unfortunately birds of prey, swans and woodpeckers have great difficulty managing with only one leg, and such birds should not be released.

Broken tail

Cats quite often plunge at birds and end up with a mouth full of tail feathers whilst the bird escapes minus its tail. Many birds get run over by cars. If a bird is not quick enough to get out of the way of a car it could get its back and wings clipped by the car. The resultant bird looks as if someone had taken a pair of scissors and cut its primary wing feathers and tail feathers. There is free movement of the tail from side to side and up and down. The bird will need to rest for at least a month. If the feathers are short or absent, so that the tail does not catch on the surroundings, then the tail bones can usually mend satisfactorily. Any long feathers should be cut. No splint in such cases is required but if bones are badly displaced or crushed a vet may need to wire them. This is a very delicate operation and usually only attempted on large birds.

Broken (and clawed /clubbed) toes

A broken toe can be recognized by its unnatural positon, the inability of the bird to move its toe and grip, and by feeling the break. Clawed/clubbed toes are akin to a clenched fist. The toes are bent backwards in a clenched position. One or all the toes may be curled into a ball and there may be some swelling. This condition, along with broken toes, can be treated easily and usually successfully.

(ABOVE)A little 'shoe' can help a bird greatly. It is most important for a bird to be able to stand and balance well.

(BELOW) The 'shoe'.

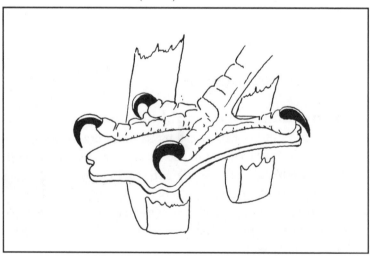

Look at the size of the bird's toes and make it a shoe out of a plastic food container such as a margarine tub. Cut out a Y shape. Ease the toes gently back into the correct positions and then the claws can be placed through nicks in the plastic. The shoe is fastened in place with micropore tape which is wrapped around it. Keep the shoe on the bird for two weeks.

Sometimes baby birds get their feet clogged up with dirt and excreta. Young birds' feet are very delicate. Soak the feet in water before removing the debris.

This heron had a very badly broken wing and was emaciated.

Broken wings

Broken wings usually droop and the breaks are relatively easy to locate. If the skin is broken, then disinfect the wound as explained in the section on cuts and bites (see below). Then fold the wing into its natural position. Strap the wing into place, folded, using surgical tape (micropore tape is suitable for small birds. Use zinc oxide plaster for large birds).

There are several methods of strapping wings but the following two methods are usually adequate.

(a) For small birds the tape can go in front of the legs and under the wing which is not broken.

(b) For large birds, pass the tape around the wing tip first, and then in front of the legs and under the uninjured wing.

Whatever method is used, most birds will have some difficulty in balancing. Small birds may fall over onto their backs and not be able to turn over, especially if they have long tails. Consequently, it is necessary to keep a close eye on birds that have had their wings strapped up and it may be best to keep such birds in a confined and well padded space.

The tape should be kept in place for about ten days for minor breaks in small birds. For very severe breaks in large birds it may be necessary to keep the wing strapped in place for up to four weeks. It is usually quite easy to remove the tape. Just cut it with sharp scissors. Don't worry if a few feathers come off.

Sometimes where there has been an open wound (as in a compound fracture) tissue grows to form a hard calous mass — rather like a corn — which prevents flight. This may disappear when treated with Dermisol cream.

Cuts and bites

Birds that have been attacked by cats frequently die of septi-

(ABOVE) Methods of bandaging wings.

(BELOW)This blackbird was in very poor condition and had a break at the humerous/radius/ulna joint.

(ABOVE) Cuts should be bathed daily.

(OPPOSITE ABOVE) Sometimes nestlings get their feet caught up in nesting materials. Hold the bird gently but firmly and cut away all debris.

(OPPOSITE BELOW) Wounds at the tops of the legs are common following attacks by cats.

caemia. This is often called the 'three-day syndrome' as the birds look as if they are recovering but die within three days. Except for very nervous birds, and robins, which tend to react badly to antibiotic injections, an injection should be given to help to prevent septicaemia.

Antibiotics may also be given by mouth, especially in the case of larger birds. If giving a tablet, push it right down the back of the throat. The rounded end of a paintbrush or pill-giver may be useful for this, depending on the size of the birds, but it is better to conceal a tablet in a small piece of food which is fed to the bird. Antibiotics are usually given to small birds in drinking water or as treated seed. When antibiotics are added

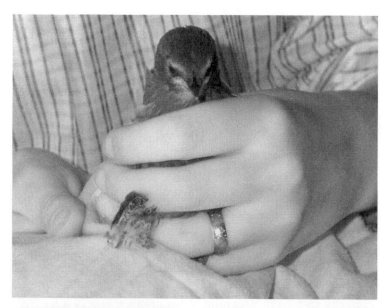

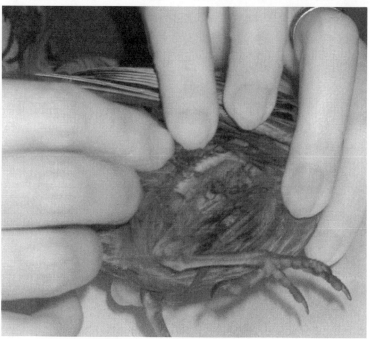

to drinking water or food it is more difficult to control the dose.

All traumatized birds can be given aconite and arnica.

Cuts and bites must be kept clean. Bathe and disinfect them once a day for the first four to six days, as necessary. A standard antiseptic solution can be bought from a pet shop. Follow the instructions on the bottle. Cuts and bites should be attended to immediately and if such an antiseptic solution is not available then any human antiseptic solution for cuts and grazes can be used — or you can use salt water. Follow the instructions on the bottle and treat as you would for a child.

Keep the bird warm. It is inadvisable to house a bird with an open wound in an aviary. Do not leave the bird outside at night for at least seven days. (Refer to the section on housing, p. 73)

In the case of shot wounds consult your vet. The feathers should be removed from shot wounds but the pellets can be left if they are too deep. The pellets may eventually be removed if you treat with Dermisol cream (available from veterinary clinics). Pick the feathers out of the wound using sterile tweezers. You can sterilize utensils using a baby bottle sterilizer — or just boil them or heat over a flame until red hot and allow to cool. If you use Dermisol cream, the shot will work its way to the surface and can be removed along with other debris as you regularly clean the wound.

Even quite large cuts may heal if you pack them with Dermisol cream, but for deep cuts, exposing internal organs, suturing is a must. Consult your vet.

Dislocations

Dislocations in humans are common at the shoulder. In birds they can occur at the 'elbow' and 'wrist' of the wing. They can also occur in the leg. They can be distinguished from fractures of the joints by feeling the displaced bones, which will have rounder ends than those of a fracture. It is possible to manipulate the bones back into place, but they may recur. The movement of a break is generally more free, and the limb is held outwards at an awkward angle. However, it is best to leave the decision, and any manipulation of a dislocation, to a vet.

Drowning/wet/chilled birds

Most birds can swim to some extent. Sometimes garden birds will fall into ponds when bathing on water lilies. If the pond does not have a sloping or stepped edge, and the bird cannot get out of the water, it will die within about twenty minutes.

If the bird has stopped breathing, hold it upside down and open its mouth for a minute to allow the water to drain away. Gently press the breast bone every 3 - 5 seconds if the heart has stopped beating.

Birds that have almost died will make a complete recovery in about an hour using the following technique. Mop off the excess water. Hold the bird in the hand for about twenty minutes, or put it on a source of heat, such as a warm hot-water bottle or heating pad. *Do not overheat.* As with humans, hypothermia requires gentle treatment. The peripheral blood supply is shut down and excessive direct heat will result in a rush of blood to the peripheries and away from the vital organs. A condition similar to frost bite might also occur.

After about twenty minutes the bird should start standing up. It may shiver violently, and tuck its head into its feathers. After a further 10 - 20 minutes it will become more aware of its surroundings and will — in the case of nearly drowning — mess.

Once it has reached this stage it is well on its way to recovery and it will probably start to preen itself. It will try to distance itself from you, but *do not let it go until it can fly adequately (for example, across a room).* Crows, birds of prey, cats and foxes will wait near ponds for such casualties. Once the bird can fly well, it should be released. Many of the birds that are rescued from ponds are fledglings which have followed their parents to the water. After releasing such birds, wait, or return after an hour or so to ensure that their parents have found them. If the parents don't reappear, you may have to take over. Soaking wet ducklings are sometimes found, and should be taken into care. This may happen if they have lost their mothers

Casualties will mostly be found in the mornings about 10 - 12 noon on hot days in May - July. If bird casualties are found regularly in a pond, think about altering the design of the pond to prevent this. Garden ponds with steep sides and/or lips are death-traps for birds. A concrete or wooden slope, or even a flowerpot or piece of chicken wire in each corner could save the lives of many birds. Better still, convert traditional ponds into wildlife ponds. The site should be kept open so that cats cannot hide at the edge of the pond.

Use similar rescue techniques for all birds found wet and chilled. However birds that are found wet, cold and unable to fly during bad winter months are usually in very poor condition and may be starving. Such birds should be kept for at least two weeks. Test water birds for waterproofing before release, by trying them in a large tub or bath.

Chilled waterfowl are sometimes found, which have lost their waterproofing. This may be because the bird has not preened itself, which could be due to disease, poisoning or injury. Such birds are usually very poorly.

Or, the oil gland that waterfowl use to preen themselves may have become clogged. This gland is above the tail, on the back, and looks a bit like a pimple. If it seems to be swollen, inflamed and blocked, then gently bathe it and massage it with cooking oil. Repeat several times a day for a few days and then the hard plug blocking it may be removed. If this doesn't work, consult a vet.

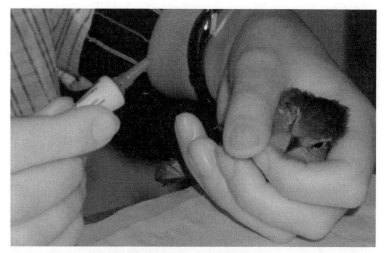

When the bird blinks the ointment will be distributed over the eye.

Extremely sick birds

A bird that is dying usually pants heavily, cannot stand and may close its eyes. Fits may occur, and the bird may gasp every minute or so. Keep the bird warm and quiet. A heating pad or warm hot-water bottle is suitable. Supply a darkened area for it to hide away. Give it sugar water if you are experienced at doing this (refer to the section on feeding). Also give carbo-vegitabilis and arnica (see section on homoeopathy).

Eyes

If a bird's eyes are closed this could be due to an infection, or to dust and foreign bodies penetrating and inflaming the eyes. Newly hatched songbirds have their eyes closed. They should be fully open when the bird is feathered. Occasionally the eyes do not open and the bird is expelled from the nest. Bathe the eyes in warm water as you would for a child. Repeat four or five times during the day. If the eyes still do not open, try gently easing the eyelids apart whilst bathing them in a diluted eye solution. If this still does not work, seek veterinary assistance.

(ABOVE) This fledgling was caught by a cat. It had just left the nest but could not fly because of grossly malformed feathers.

(OPPOSITE ABOVE) A bird may be unable to fly after only a few of the flight feathers have been damaged.

(OPPOSITE BELOW) Underside of a wing and outline of feather.

Sticky or glazed eyes are indicative of an infection (refer to sections on disease and parasites).

For ulcers of the eye, your vet can give you suitable eye ointment. Unfortunately, ulcers can be difficult to treat successfully.

Some one-eyed birds can be released, but not birds of prey. All birds rely heavily on eyesight and any trouble with the eyes will obviously diminish their chances of survival. Cases for release need to be assessed individually.

Feathers

If a bird has not been feeding properly it may develop fault bars in its feathers. These are small breaks or marks in the vanes

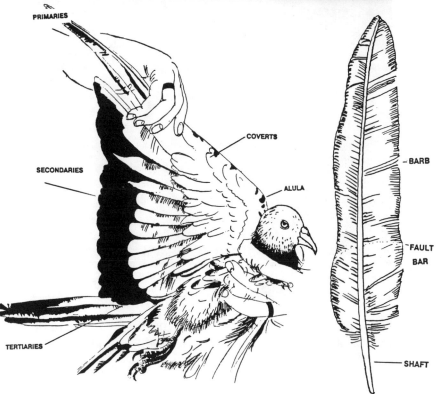

PRIMARIES

COVERTS

SECONDARIES

ALULA

TERTIARIES

BARB

FAULT BAR

SHAFT

This wood pigeon arrived in very poor condition. It could not fly. Notice the shortness of the wings compared with the tail, indicating missing primary feathers.

of the feathers. Usually they are not much of a problem, but they could be so severe that they prevent the bird from flying as it should. Birds that have been hand-reared since their first days of life may develop deformed feathers if they have been fed on a poor diet.

Bare patches on the chest, head and back may be caused by mite infestation. These can be eradicated easily by using a bird insect spray or powder (refer to section on parasites).

If the flight feathers (primary and secondary feathers) of the wing are damaged, then the bird will not be able to fly. Badly damaged feathers will be removed by the bird, and new ones take one or two months to grow long enough for flight. If the quills have been severed they may have haemorrhaged and the bird could be in very poor condition. Feathers, and the tail, will re-grow, given time; a balanced diet, with plenty of variety, helps. If the tail is broken, the bird will need at least

Wryneck in a bird is a bad sign, indicating that the bird is very ill.

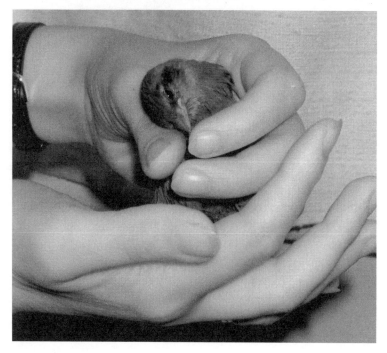

This baby blackbird could not hold its head up properly to gape and had to be supported in order to be fed.

a month of rest. Length of recovery varies with time of year — birds usually moult after the breeding season, so this is a good time for regrowing feathers. Providing a daily bird bath will encourage the bird to preen and remove defective feathers.

Going light

Some birds lose weight rapidly as a result of illness, but 'going light' refers to birds that do not feed easily and die within a few days or weeks. Such birds just do not seem to have the will to live. They dislike being handled, hide in a corner and fade away. Always suspect worms (and external parasites) and treat accordingly (see section on parasites).

In the absence of any outward signs of disease or injury, it would be impossible to tell whether a bird had an illness or

It could only hold its head up straight for a few minutes at a time; when it was tired the head flopped down. By the time the blackbird was a couple of months old, however, all signs of the problem with the neck had disappeared.

This moorhen was hit in the side and head by a car. Notice the twisted head. It had concussion, a broken wing and a broken leg. It recovered.

was 'moping' unless a full veterinary examination was carried out. Some birds just do not take to captivity at all well. They can be literally frightened to death, whilst others of the same species recover well from severe injuries. This is sometimes referred to as 'capture myopathy'.

Head injuries

Head injuries may occur when a bird falls from a nest or when it flies into a closed window (see section on stunned birds, p. 44). The head may be held sideways or upside down (called 'wryneck'), indicating brain damage or severe concussion resulting from an accident. Unnatural positioning of the head may also be indicative of disease, or vitamin deficiency (niacin) resulting in a condition similar to pellagra. Pellagra is a vitamin deficiency and is characterized in humans by weakness, and sometimes dermatitis and diarrhoea and nervous system defects. It is not well documented in wild birds and I believe this to be the first reported case (in this book) in a very young blackbird, where the bird was successfully hand-reared and returned to the wild. The only symptom was severe wryneck.. The photographs on pages 34 and 35 show the bird's development and its recovery from the illness. The illness is thought to arise from an unbalanced diet — in this case it was likely that the baby blackbird had been fed by its parents on a predominantly bread diet. The bird was reared on recipe 2 (see p. 63) with ¼ teaspoon SA37 (see p. 93) daily, and mincemeat. It received a multivitamin injection on days 5, 12 and 19 after arrival. It was approximately five days old when it arrived. It was overwintered in an aviary and by the time it was released, the following spring, the wryneck had almost completely disappeared.

If the problem is a disease rather than a vitamin deficiency or an accident, then it will get progressively worse and there will usually be other indicators — the bird will not be bright, it will be dull, reluctant to preen and unable to follow your movements with its head; it may have diarrhoea. If the bird is bright and chirpy and eating well, then it is telling you that it is doing fine.

For head problems, isolate the bird and keep it in a quiet, warm place. Give it antibiotics (obtainable from your vet) and vitamins. If it shows no signs of recovery after a few weeks, and appears to be getting worse, or if it is considerably distressed, then euthanasia may be best.

A bird may also hang its head sideways because of impaction of the oesophagus or because of an air sac, and botulism may cause the head to hang down (refer to section below and on pp. 15 and 51).

Unconscious birds may have their eyes open. If this is the case then the eyes must be moistened several times a day.

Impaction
Crop/gizzard/oesophagus impaction

Sometimes birds eat things that they cannot digest and that will remain in the crop/gizzard or oesophagus and cause a feeding blockage. The bird will be listless and cannot feed. This is often referred to as 'sour crop'. This condition may result from inexperienced feeding of baby birds — frequently feeding too much bread, which expands when wet and regularly blocks the crop.

Roundworms can also cause a blockage (see p. 55).

This baby pigeon died from impaction of the oesophagus. Notice the swelling in the neck and the bloated (but empty) crop.

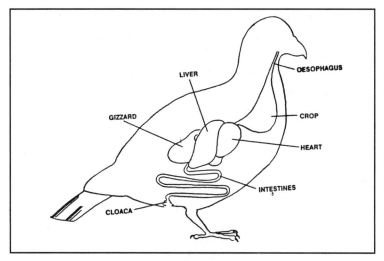

Outline of the digestive tract.

If the obstruction is in the oesophagus (food pipe) or in the back of the throat, the bird may thrust its head forward, open its beak widely, and move its neck as if to swallow every few minutes. You may be able to remove the obstruction with round-ended tweezers, if you can see it.

If the obstruction is further down, give the bird cod liver oil, a drop at a time. (Small birds can have 3 - 5 drops — about ½ inch in a dropper — and large birds can have up to 10 drops.) Repeat twice at half-hourly intervals, and massage gently.

If the obstruction still remains, consult your vet as the blockage will either need to be squeezed up to the throat and out of the mouth or removed surgically.

Pigeons sometimes present with fluid in the crop. This can be dealt with similarly by turning the bird upside down and squeezing the crop gently to expel the fluid. In this case, however, the prognosis is usually poor as copious fluid is indicative of advanced infection.

Cloacal impaction

All adult birds should be given a source of water to drink, but some waterbirds will only mess when on water and therefore should be given a large supply of water. Grebes, divers, gannets, razorbills and guillemots occasionally suffer from cloacal impaction, when they do not have access to water: due to an accumulation of urates which results in constipation. It is not easy to diagnose, but sometimes the extended cloaca can be seen and felt. The bird will be reluctant to move and will strain. Give the bird cod liver oil on food (about 10 drops every half hour for a day) and seek veterinary advice if this does not work.

Egg bound

Birds sometimes become egg bound. This is where the bird has not been able to lay an egg, and the egg is retained in the body. Birds that are egg bound are reluctant to move and can be seen straining. They will die within about a day if not treated.

The usual treatment is to slightly force the egg out by opening the vent. Feel for the egg by gently pressing the abdomen. Then apply pressure at the top of the egg to open the vent slightly. Apply cooking oil. Relax pressure, and then apply pressure again to force the egg out. If this does not work, an operation will be necessary.

Inability to stand

Although birds are noted for standing on one leg, some birds will not stand or fly if one leg is injured.

If the legs are not injured, inability to stand could be due to any form of illness resulting in acute weakness (or synovitis). It is one of the symptoms of fowl paralysis (Newcastle disease or paramyxovirus) in pigeons. However, in small birds, it is usually due to internal injuries, resulting from being squashed in the hand, or being attacked by a cat. Such birds need isolation and intensive nursing. They may need to be force fed and their prognosis is poor. Seek veterinary assistance if disease is suspected, and suspect spinal injury (p. 43).

Young pigeons and large birds may be unable to stand if they are starving.

Oiled birds

Seabirds can become covered in oil when there is an accident involving an oil tanker. The same also applies to inland birds. Furthermore, many people keep oil in their garages and birds sometimes have mishaps with trays of oil left lying around.

Wipe the eyes and beak as necessary with damp cotton wool. Then wash the bird in washing-up liquid. Do this as soon as possible because oil is poisonous and the longer the bird is left, the longer it will try to clean itself and thereby ingest the poison. However, if the bird is very poorly, for example starving and hypothermic, then its condition will need to be stabilized first. Only reasonably fit birds will attempt to clean themselves. Each bird will need to be assessed individually.

Use washing-up liquid — Fairy liquid is suitable. The water must be hand hot (about 40-42°C). Have two buckets of hand-hot soapy water and one bucket of hand-hot rinsing water ready. Look at the bird and note the heavily soiled areas. Immerse the bird up to its neck. The oiled feathers should be rubbed and the head can be cleaned very gently with a toothbrush. Tip heavily soiled water away and repeat the process. Open the wings and wash underneath the wings as necessary. Rinse the bird thoroughly. A shower attachment is necessary so that the water can be jetted onto the plumage until it begins to drip off. Mop off the excess water and put the bird near a heater to dry and preen itself.

Remove tar and grease with Swarfega or other non-toxic hand cleaner which can be bought from a hardware store.

If the bird shows signs of poisoning, for example lethargy or inability to preen itself, then the usual treatment is 1 - 6 ml

41

of a product containing kaolin which is available from your vet (use 1 ml for small birds) followed by fluid therapy (Lectade is often used) and one teaspoon liquid paraffin for four days (see section on poisoning).

It is advisable to feed poisoned birds on non-abrasive food for a few days because ingested oil causes inflammation of the digestive tract.

All birds will be de-oiled after washing and they should be kept under observation after washing and not released immediately.

Most seabirds become waterproof again within a day or two. Do not release any bird until you are sure it is waterproof and able to fly. Encourage bathing, which in turn encourages preening. Preening is necessary in order for the bird to become fully waterproofed.

Racing pigeons

Birds will just drop to the ground due to hunger and/or exhaustion. Check birds for injuries. A racing pigeon that is just hungry and exhausted will usually recover fully within a few weeks.

The owner can usually be traced by the bird's ring number. The owner is obliged to take the bird but will probably not want an injured bird or one that raced badly. As an alternative, you could keep the bird to recuperate for about six months, after which time it may 'home in' on its new surroundings. It will probably return daily for some time and it should be given food and be allowed back into the aviary as necessary (see section on releasing, p. 90).

Removing hooks and lines

If a piece of line is hanging from the mouth, then knot immediately to a long length of line. Pass this through a length of tubing which is longer than the bird's neck but narrow enough to pass down its throat. For swans a one-centimetre diameter tube is suitable. Lubricate the tubing with cooking oil. Slide the tube down the throat until it meets resistance. Then gently push the hook free and pull on the line so that the tubing and hook are expelled from the mouth. This process should be carried out under the guidance of a vet. On no account should the hook be forced out.

If the hook does not slide out without resistance, an X-ray may be necessary. If the hook is lodged in the gizzard, it is sometimes left, if the bird is still able to feed; or an operation may be required. It depends on whether lead is involved (see section on poisons, p. 52)

Then feed the bird (but not too much in the first meal).

Spasms of the side

The bird collapses and jerks; rhythmic jerking may occur on only one side; the beak opens, the eye may blink, the wing jerks down and the foot jerks up. The spasms may occur many times per minute. There are no droppings. This condition may result from sudden chilling causing cramps.

Wrap the bird up and keep it warm. Give it about 5 drops (or ¼ inch in a dropper) of sugar water (sugar, or preferably glucose, dissolved in water) and 5 drops (or ¼ inch in a dropper) of cod liver oil every half hour until the bird messes and starts to recover. Because of the spasms, ensure that the liquid passes right down the throat.

Seizures may result from poisoning. It is always advisable to consult a vet when seizures/spasms occur, if the above treatment does not work.

Spine and nerve injuries

If an injured bird reacts as if it has more than one broken limb (for instance, both wings are drooping, or it is unable to use both legs, usually lying on its belly), but no breaks can be found, then it probably has spinal damage. Sometimes a damaged peripheral nerve will result in symptoms akin to a broken limb. A bad cut may cause this. Birds can sustain sprains, strains and torn ligaments and muscles, all of which can result in the inability to move a limb. If the wings or legs are hanging out of place, then they must be strapped up as in the case of broken bones, otherwise the bird will flap around and do more damage to itself. Keep the bird in a quiet, warm place.

If there is slight damage to the spine (for instance, a slipped disc), then this may heal.

If the bird does not recover within a couple of weeks, or if it is in considerable distress, then euthanasia may be best.

Stunned birds/birds that cannot fly

Birds sometimes fly into closed windows, hit their heads and suffer concussion. In particular, birds of prey sometimes crash into closed windows. They fall to the ground and just sit there. No treatment is necessary and they usually recover fully after two to three weeks in an aviary (but see also section on head injuries, p. 36).

If young birds that have been reared by hand are unable to fly, this is usually due to malnutrition resulting in weakness. Such birds will normally start to fly after a few months on a balanced diet (see p. 56).

Sometimes birds are found sitting in roads or gardens. This is quite common in winter and at migration times, when the birds may just not be able to fly any more due to hunger and/or exhaustion. They may have passed right underneath a car, and/or hit their heads and be stunned. Such birds usually make a full recovery in a few weeks. If a bird has been trapped in a shed or rescued from a chimney, then it may not be able to fly. No treatment is necessary but it should be well cared for.

During bad weather birds may roost in a torpid state. Gently warm them up (see section on wet/chilled birds, p. 27).

This kingfisher has a badly fractured wing, bad news for a bird that relies on its wings for diving.

They may also drop to the ground due to disease. Sometimes swifts miss their annual migration. It is best to keep them until the spring, but you will have to hand feed swifts, swallows and house martins as these birds feed whilst on the wing. Swifts and swallows may also land by mistake. They will be able to take off if you hold them out in your hand and flick them gently upwards. Do this over something soft in case they drop to the ground.

Sometimes birds such as geese land in small gardens by mistake; such birds need a 'runway' so that they can take off. Give the birds food and water and take them to an open area after ensuring that there is no other reason why they should not fly.

Seabirds often come inland during bad weather and then drop due to hunger. They can be 'fattened up' and released in more clement weather. If they are strictly seabirds and have been blown inland then when they are ready for release take them back to the coast. If you need to keep larger seabirds for some time — many months — then it may be worthwhile considering taking them to a sanctuary that has large tanks.

3 DISEASES, POISONS AND PARASITES

DISEASES

Symptoms of disease in birds include difficulty in breathing, loss of appetite, weight loss, listlessness, diarrhoea, fever (as detected by the warmth of the feet and beak), cloudy eyes, sticky eyes and beak, discharge from the mouth, nose and/or ears, lesions in the mouth, unnatural positioning of the head (sideways or upside down) and shivering.

Unnatural behaviour is normally the first sign of illness, and healthy birds do not pant or make marked movements of the breast when breathing.

You may find a bird that is diseased; or it may arise as a complication of injuries, and the confinement of birds together. Consequently, all birds should be checked regularly for any signs of disease, even when aviaries are kept scrupulously clean.

If you suspect that a bird is suffering from an infectious disease, keep it isolated and seek veterinary asistance as soon as possible. The external signs of many diseases are non-specific and they cannot be fully identified without laboratory tests. Tuberculosis, salmonella, fowl paralysis, avian cholera and psittacosis are some of the diseases that birds may suffer from.

Tuberculosis is unlikely to be transmitted to man from birds, but the possibility exists. The psittacosis organism causes penumonia in humans, and the salmonella organism can cause paratyphoid in humans.

This sparrow developed a large air sac under its skin after being attacked by a cat.

An injured wild bird may develop septicaemia/synovitis syndrome, which is treated by broad spectrum antibiotics. The signs are swelling of the joints (particularly noticeable at the hock), lameness and high body temperature. Bumblefoot is a swelling on the foot which may result from a cut on the foot pad.

Without confirmation of the type of disease, the vet will usually prescribe a broad spectrum antibiotic. Penicillins or tetracyclines are usually used. Chloramphenicol, streptomycin or nitrofurans may be used if the condition persists. Acute disease is usually followed by rapid death if the condition is not alleviated within a few days. Therefore, injection is usually advisable and this can be followed by a course of tablets.

Symptoms sometimes reappear after a couple of weeks, indicating the need for a further course of antibiotics.

Birds being treated for disease should be isolated and kept warm. They may need hand feeding.

For conditions such as canker and coccoidosis sometimes suitable medication can be obtained from pet suppliers. However, it is always wise to consult a vet.

The brief list on p. 49 gives an idea of some of the symptoms to look out for in the first examination for common and *infectious diseases*. If you had a pet bird you would notice, for instance, when it stopped singing, if its voice sounded funny, it could not hear you, could not see very well, refused to fly, was reluctant to move, kept drinking, stopped eating, if its feathers fell out or it plucked them out, if it started flying into things or was reluctant to preen.

There are many conditions of course which are not infectious. Birds may have congenital defects. They may have a heart attack, or a perforated intestine or gizzard. They may possibly have tumours (but these things are rarely diagnosed in birds).

Viral diseases

There is usually no magic treatment for viral diseases. The usual method of eradicating killer viral diseases from flocks is isolation and euthanasia of infected birds, followed by meticulous cleaning of infected areas and immunization where possible.

Diseases such as duck plague (characterized mainly by general wasting), parvovirus, paramyxovirus (fowl paralysis) and picornavirus (avian hepatitis) are all viral diseases. Birds sometimes catch colds and with warmth and care a quick recovery can be expected. Medication for colds can be obtained from pet shops and vets.

Bacterial and other diseases

Bacterial diseases such as salmonellosis are often treated successfully with antibiotics. However, birds suspected of having avian cholera and tuberculosis are usually euthanased.

Infections of *Pasteurella anatipestifer* and *Erysipelothrix rhusiopathiae* can occur and species of *Actinobacillus* and *Mycoplasma* are important infectious agents. Psittacosis, which is a well known disease of pigeons, is caused by the organism

Chlamydia psittaci. In this case, bathe the eyes several times a day with a weak solution of boric acid, as well as giving antibiotic.. sing; however, usually birds with psittacosis are euthanased.

Besides the organisms mentioned above, the other main groups of organism causing diseases in birds are parasites and fungi. Parasites are considered in a separate section (see p. 53). The main fungal infection of birds is aspergillosis, but other fungal infections can occur. Suitable medication can be obtained from a vet.

Toxins

Some organisms produce substances that are poisonous to birds. The bird can become ill after eating or drinking substances containing the toxin excreted by the organisms (exotoxins). Sometimes the organism retains the toxin (endotoxins) and the bird becomes ill after the bacteria multiply and produce the toxin inside the bird. There is a separate section dealing with poisoning.

Listed below are some of the symptoms which may present, along with possible causes:

Difficulty in breathing
accompanied by loss of appetite and listlessness
    aspergillosis, or pneumonia
accompanioed by scabs on the feet and beak
    avian pox
accompanied by nasal discharge and swollen eyelids
    mycoplasma infection (birds of prey are susceptible to this)
accompanied by wart-like skin nodules
    tuberculosis

Vomiting and/or diarrhoea with pungent smell
salmonellosis, coliform infections, duck plague (which affects ducks, geese and swans)
accompanied by purulent nasal discharge and conjunctivities
Psittacosis(roup or ornithosis) (this is common in poultry, geese, ducks, pigeons and doves)
accomapnied by lack of co-ordination, wryneck and leg paralysis in pigeons
fowl paralysis (Newcastle disease or paramyxovirus)

Fever
accompanied by swelling of the joints
   synovitis (usually caused by staphylococcus infections)

Slime in the mouth
   canker (this is most common in squabs — young pigeons in the nest)

NB *Some or all the symptoms may appear in the case of each disease.*

POISONS

Mercury, cadmium, copper, zinc and vanadium poisoning could also occur. Again there is usually progressive weakness. The severity of the symptoms depends upon the amount of poison absorbed, and death will result from severe poisoning.

Mycotoxins are toxins from moulds, and this sort of poisoning may result from eating contaminated food. Outbreaks of aflatoxin poisoning and ergotism can occur in flocks feeding on mouldy grain.

Sudden large-scale deaths of birds should be reported to your local environmental health officer and the Ministry of Agriculture, Fisheries and Food. Poisoning should be suspected. A very bad outbreak of an infectious disease might also result in large-scale deaths, but a sudden occurrence is usually associated with poisoning. Birds can act as indicators of contamination and dangers to humans, and therefore, if contamination is suspected, dead birds should be given to your local health officer for analysis.

In an emergency, and without knowing the type of poison, cold tea or a charcoal solution (available from your vet) can be given. Fluids should only be given to a bird by an experienced person, because of the danger of drowning (see section on feeding). Poisoned birds should be kept warm and given plenty of fluids.

The usual treatment for poisoning (as for oiled birds) is 1 - 6 ml of a product containing kaolin . Your vet will be able to supply and advise about the dose. This is usually followed by rehydration fluid for four days (1 tablespoon sugar, and 1 teaspoon salt made up to 1 litre with water).Give three 10 ml doses each day for crow sized birds. If it is necessary to force feed the bird on a liquid diet then the rehydration fluid is unnecessary.

Botulism, caused by the multiplication of bacteria in water during hot summers, can kill birds. Waterfowl are particularly susceptible. The illness results from a bacterial toxin so basically the bird is suffering from poisoning. Botulism also occurs in humans and therfore caution is needed. Infected birds may hold their heads down as paralysis occurs. The legs and wings may also be affected; they may have a greenish diarrhoea, which is not very smelly. Birds suffering from botulism often need hand feeding, because of paralysis of the neck; they also need plenty of fluids. Again, follow the usual treatment for poisoning given above. There is an antitoxin for botulism, but it is not always effective.

Algae and fungal blooms in lakes can also lead to outbreaks of poisoning.

Lead poisoning is still common in waterfowl. Lead poisoning results in progressive weakness, lethargy, green liquid faeces, emaciation and ataxia. Very little can be done but chelating

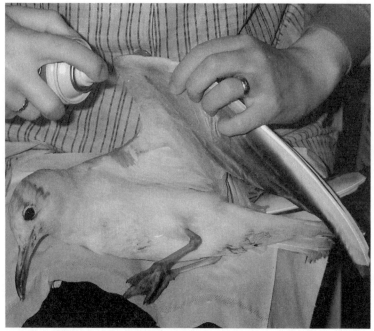

Some newly arrived birds may be heavily infected with parasites. Treat all new arrivals with a bird insecticide.

agents ('mopping up' agents) may help, and recovery can be expected for mild cases. With ducks, they quite often cannot hold their heads up to feed; in the case of swans, their necks are often kinked. Swallowed lead can be removed surgically. This may be necessary if the bird has swallowed a fishing line. Sometimes the lead can be extracted via the throat using a powerful magnet, whilst the bird is anaesthetized and supported upside down. If lead poisoning is suspected, consult your vet.

PARASITES

Parasites are found on and in healthy birds and are only problematic when the host's resistance is low and the numbers of parasites increase excessively. Wild birds control external parasites (ectoparasites) that live on their feathers and skin by bathing, preening, anting and by the use of millipedes, which they use in the same way as ants. Ants and millipedes (especially pill millipedes) exude a toxin that will kill many external parasites. Many wild bird parasites can infest domestic animals such as dogs.

Avoid handling birds with external parasites. Never touch external parasites. Biting insects can cause disease. Ticks can cause Lyme Disease.

Parasites can be grouped as follows:

external parasites	mites and ticks
	lice and fleas
	flies
internal parasites	worms — roundworms, tapeworms, flukeworms, spiny headed worms
	other organisms

External parasites may cause the eyes to become swollen and sore and they may close completely.

Some external parasite infections can easily be treated with insecticides. However, it is always advisable to consult a vet when internal parasites are suspected.

Use a general insecticide spray/powder designed specially for birds when it is necessary to control fleas, lice, hippoboscids and other flies, and always treat new arrivals.

Leeches may sometimes cause problems for waterfowl. Remove them with tweezers.

EXTERNAL PARASITES

Mites

Mites can cause scaly face and feet, which become swollen and deformed. Apply an edible oil, such as olive oil, to the feet. Mites can also cause bare patches to appear on the chest, head and back. Suitable insecticides are available from pet shops and veterinary practices. Some are very specific, such as feather rot cream for bald patches.

Mites resemble minute spiders.

Ticks

Ticks can be removed with tweezers after dabbing them with cooking oil or butter and waiting for them to die. Species of *Ixodes* look like black/blue grains of rice after feeding. Look for ticks on the head and neck.

Lice

Lice can easily be seen as they come to the surface of the feathers when you hold the bird for a few minutes in your hands. They will be seen when you lift up your gloved hands. They look like minute silver fish, and wood pigeons are particularly susceptible to them.

Blowfly maggots

Blowfly maggots found in open wounds can be removed with tweezers or flushed out with soapy water.

Internal Parasites

Roundworms and tapeworms

Roundworms and tapworms can be diagnosed by looking for eggs and segments in the droppings, which are often frothy. Suitable medication can be obtained from pet suppliers as well as vets, but it is always wise to consult a vet. Suspect worms if the bird is 'going light', sneezing and wheezing and/or periodically panting. Routinely deworm all in-house birds.

Gape

Gape can be caused by a form of roundworm found in the bird's trachea (windpipe). It can affect garden birds and pigeons, as well as pheasants. The bird will be listless, and every few minutes it will thrust its head forward, open its beak widely and move its neck as if to swallow. The bird may cough after it gapes. These symptoms may also occur if there is another type of blockage in the throat. Specific anti-gape treatments are available from veterinary surgeons and animal health suppliers. Affected birds may need to be hand fed.

Canker

Canker is also sometimes called gape or protozoal infection. The symptoms are similar to those for roundworms in the throat. However, a slimy white/yellow substance in the mouth and throat is very characteristic of canker. It is easily treated when not too far advanced. Suitable medication can be obtained from large pet stores and from vets. Trichomonad species are the normal causative agents, but other types of protozoa can cause canker, including coccidia species; therefore different medication is sometimes necessary. Affected birds may need to be hand fed.

4 FEEDING

If a feathered garden bird is very sickly, give it some sugar water. Dissolve some sugar (or preferaby glucose) in a small amount of water and drip one drop onto the side of the bird's beak using a finger, paintbrush, dropper or syringe. The bird should swallow it. If it does not swallow it, do not try again. If the bird does swallow it, offer one or two more drops.

Do not attempt this if you are unsure as it is very easy to drown a bird.

Listless larger birds such as crows, seagulls, etc, which are too weak to feed, can initially be given a rehydration fluid (see section on poisons, p. 51). Give 5 - 10 ml using a feeding tube. *Avoid giving birds milk.*

BABY BIRDS

Avoid giving baby birds cold/chilled foods. Food should be at room temperature or tepid, otherwise stunted growth may result.

Do not give baby garden birds seeds or roughage. Baby birds fed on an unnatural diet may accumulate seed kernels in the crop, which leads to digestive problems.

Unfeathered birds will usually need feeding during the night for the first one to two weeks. A contented baby bird will usually sleep between meals. A hungry bird will become very active and then slump when it begins to starve.

If a newly arrived young garden bird such as a sparrow is happy to sit on your hand, then it is almost certainly unable to feed itself.

Feathered birds will feed during daylight hours and if this is adequate they will sleep through the night. However, if a bird is found in the evening, it will be necessary to feed it during the night. A hungry bird may call and beg for food even in the dark. If a bird is going to die in the night, it will usually do so in the early hours of the morning, particularly if the temperature is allowed to drop. As a general rule, feed all baby birds the first night - by force if necessary.

Great care is necessary when feeding baby birds. The aim must always be to get the food well past the glottis (this is the opening leading to the lungs) and down the back of the throat.

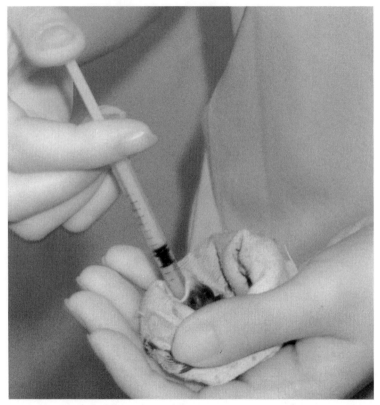

Take care only to give very young birds a small amount of food at a time.

Slide the dropper (an eye dropper can be bought from a chemist) or syringe (a vet may be able to give you one) down the roof of the mouth until it will not go any further without being forced.

Small pieces of solid food such as lean mince can be fed to a bird using a matchstick or a pair of round-ended tweezers. Stamp tweezers are usually suitable. You must ensure that the food is positioned correctly at the back of the mouth, otherwise it will lie in the mouth and the bird may choke. The recipes can be fed using sticks or a syringe, depending on how much water is added. Let the bird guide you as to how much food it needs. Birds that gape will soon let you know when they are hungry. Some birds require encouragement to gape, particularly those that have been found after they have left the nest, and some birds will need to be force fed until they are self-sufficient. Pigeons do not gape.

Tiny nestlings with their eyes not yet open can be encouraged to gape by touching the beak or by putting them about 33 centimetres from a lamp (avoid the glare) and then putting your hand over the lamp to create a shadow. Alternatively, you could try gently shaking their box, leaving them in a dark box for a few minutes, or imitating a bird sound. Cold birds may

The bird may 'hang onto' the syringe; you will need to hold it back in order to remove the syringe.

not gape. In the case of older birds, brightly coloured tweezers (red or green tape can be stuck onto the tweezers) may encourage them to peck. Once the bird begins to peck, leave some food, such as biscuit crumbs, for it to eat and increase the intervals between feeds (no longer than two hours).

Baby birds can be divided into those than can and those that can't feed themselves. Below are examples of types of birds and what they can be given to eat.

Ducks, pheasants and partridges

Ducklings will feed themselves. Feed them on chick crumbs or mash, and in an emergency porridge oats can be used. Small seeds can be added, such as millet. As they grow, the diet can be changed to poultry/duck pellets, potatoes and greens.

Pheasant and partridge chicks will eat chick crumbs and small seeds such as millet.

If a chick will not eat, try putting wetted chick crumbs

Notice the opening (glottis) to the trachea (wind pipe) which is located just behind the tongue. Food must be placed well beyond this, in the back of the throat.

Notice the swelling under the head of the bird on the left. This is natural as food is stored in the crop, and the crop should be full when the bird retires for the night.

onto its back. It may preen itself and thereby peck at the food.

Seabirds, coots, grebes, herons, crows, birds of prey
Dangle food in front of birds such as coots, grebes and birds of prey. The same approach can be used for birds that regurgitate food in front of the young, such as herons and gannets. Consequently, they can be fed on the same diet as their parents (see p. 71), but chop the food into very small pieces, and moisten as necessary.

Crows, gulls and magpies usually gape readily for food. Again, they can be fed on the same diet as their parents, moistened as necessary (see p. 71). These birds will also thrive on recipe 2 for garden birds (see p. 63) which is particularly suitable for newly hatched crows.

Garden birds, such as sparrows, starlings, finches, tits and pigeons

Scrambled and hard-boiled eggs are sometimes used to feed baby birds. An inadequate diet for a newly hatched bird may result in stunted growth and gout. Too much egg in the staple diet of hand-reared songbirds will lead to gout as the birds get older. This is characterized by inward pointing toes and mild difficulty in gripping. Severe gout can result in death. In general, gout will occur when the diet is too rich. Rickets will occur when there is a vitamin D deficiency (characterized also by inward pointing toes). A pinch of sterile bonemeal and some form of calcium supplement (for example, calcium lactate) will help to alleviate some dietary defects.

Never feed baby garden birds on bread and milk.

Some bird hospitals have produced their own recipes for baby birds. Proprietary hand rearing foods can sometimes be bought from pet shops, and these can be mixed with other ingredients such as mashed potato. If you have a successful diet for rearing birds then it is probably best to stick to it.

As individual species rear their offspring on differing diets, it is unlikely that one food would ever be ideal for all garden birds. Furthermore, the parents of some species vary the diets of their offspring as they grow. Therefore try to supplement the recipes as the birds grow.

Given below are recipes that I have found successful. They should be of a similar consistency to soft ice cream. You can make them thicker by adding less water. They may be offered on a spoon or rounded stick, but I usually use a syringe to feed baby birds. Wash the syringe daily in hot water. Wipe the bird's beak after each feed. If baby rice is not available for recipes 1 and 3, use baby cereal for babies aged from 3 - 4 months.

Recipe 1 (Baby rice food)
To ¼ cup dried baby rice (or cereal), add one teaspoon glucose or sugar, one egg yolk, a pinch of calcium lactate (from chemist), ½ teaspoon milk powder and one pinch vitamin powder, such as SA37. Mix into a smooth paste with warm water which has been previously boiled. Discard after 12 hours.

Birds fed on this recipe will produce yellowish droppings.

Recipe 2 (Beef food)
Use one cup of Hills Science Diet Feline Maintenance Formula* (dry, available from veterinary practices and some pet shops), and one jar/tin of baby beef dinner, 3 - 9 months (beef and vegetable dinners/casseroles/hotpots are all suitable).

Fill the cup of Feline Formula with previously boiled water and leave to soak for two hours in the fridge. Tip into a blender and add the beef dinner. Add about one cup of water and blend until the mixture is of soft ice cream consistency. Pour the mixture into ice cube trays and store in the freezer until it is needed. After defrosting add one pinch of bird vitamin supplement powder such as SA37. The consistency can be adjusted using dried baby rice. Discard after one day.

Recipe 3 (Baby rice/insect food)
To the same quantity of dried baby rice (or cereal), add dried insect food, soaked for two hours (e.g. dried proprietary insect food bought in pet shops as the staple diet for mynah birds) and blend with previously boiled water to form a soft paste. Add a pinch of vitamin powder, such as SA37. Discard after 12 hours.

How to use the recipes
Use recipe 1 for the first day or two after hatching because it is easily digested. However, because it is quickly digested, birds

---

* Other similar complete cat foods may also be suitable

Baby starlings are often confused with blackbirds. Notice the very prominent yellow mouth, with the bottom part of the beak much wider than the top.

fed on this diet must be fed every 2 - 3 hours during the night. Do this at night, even if they don't gape. On the day of hatching ensure that the birds are well fed. The following gives examples of how to use the recipes for specific birds.

Baby pigeons, doves and finches: start adding small quantities of proprietary rearing foods for pigeons and finches to recipe 1 when they are one or two days old. Decrease the quantity of recipe 1 as the bird grows. Also, a variety of baby foods can be added. I use dried cereal and muesli baby foods for babies from 3 or 4 months old. Two to three days after hatching you can also start adding small quantities of recipe 2 or baby beef dinners.

In an emergency, use plain baby rice, baby cereal or baby beef dinners for babies aged from 3 - 4 months.

Blackbirds, thrushes and starlings: start adding recipe 2 to recipe 1 when they are one or two days old. Replace recipe 1 with recipe 2 over the next week. Partially feathered and feathered blackbirds and thrushes do not normally like additions to recipe 2.

In an emergency it is still best to try to supply recipe 2, but baby beef dinners (for babies aged from 3 - 4 months) may be used.

Swifts, sparrows and tits: start adding small quantities of recipe 3 to recipe 1 when they are one or two days old. Replace recipe 1 with recipe 3 over a couple of days, or use with 50% baby cereal. Add some recipe 2 when they are partially feathered. Fifty per cent recipe 1 and 50% recipe 2 is suitable for birds such as wrens and sparrows from about 4 days old.

In an emergency plain baby rice can be used for sparrows and tits and baby beef dinners (for babies aged from 3 - 4 months) can be used for swifts.

Crows, magpies and jays: use recipe 2 for newly hatched birds of the corvidae family, such as crows. Then after a day or two start adding chopped adult diet as previously stated.

I have used these recipes successfully on hundreds of birds, but other rehabilitators have claimed success using a wide range of baby foods and personal recipes. Some garden birds can be sustained on biscuit (or bread) soaked in egg yolk for the first few days of life.

Once fledged, all birds should be given a variety of foods. Blue tits given proprietary insect food, mince and biscuit only were found to fly poorly when kept for several weeks. Additions to the diet such as crushed nuts, suet and sterilized bonemeal are important. Tits are very fond of cream and they can be given small quantities of it; also recipes 2 and 3, and cat/dog food and fish food.

Very difficult patients can be wrapped in material at feeding time.

A guide to the amount of food to use

size of bird	amount	feeding interval
tiny, unfeathered birds	1 - 3 x 0.2 ml (about 2 lots of ¼" in an eye dropper)	45 minutes
very small, partially feathered birds	2 - 4 x 0.3 ml (about 4 lots of ¼"in an eye dropper)	1 hour
birds the size of sparrows	2 - 4 x 0.5 ml (about 4 quarterful eye droppers)	1 hour
birds the size of blackbirds	2 - 3 x 2 ml (about 4 half-full eye droppers)	1-1½ hours
birds the size of pigeons	2 - 4 x 5 ml (about 7 full eyedroppers)Solid foods	2 hours

Solid foods

As a rough guide, a feathered blackbird will take 2 - 4 pieces of raw lean mince meat, moistened with water, every hour. Unfeathered blackbirds will take about two half pieces of mince hourly. If the food is not positioned correctly at the back of the throat, the bird will not be able to eat it.

Force feeding

Many seabirds, swifts, house martins and swallows and all baby pigeons and doves have to have their beaks prised open all the time they are in captivity (baby pigeons do not gape) and as soon as you put the food in the mouth it is usually taken readily. Some baby birds have to be force fed the first few times and this cannot be delayed for more than a couple of hours. It is a case of do it, or the bird dies.

Ease the beak open with your nails. Hold the bird in one hand, with the thumb and forefinger each side of the beak to keep it open. Then insert the dropper/syringe/piece of food with the other hand. Slide it down from the roof of the mouth as far as it will go without resistance, and ensure that it is well over the tongue and way past the glottis. Ease the head forward if it is tucked in, so that the neck is reasonably straight. A feeding tube is necessary if the bird is not fully conscious, or has neck paralysis, and when rehydration fluids need to be given. The tube must be gently passed down the back of the throat as far as it will go without resistance.

If you are unsure about giving liquid food, ask for guidance and feed only small amounts at each attempt. It is very easy to drown a bird with liquid food. If you are using solid food only, dip every other piece in water.

Fish eaters often regurgitate food. If they do, just feed them again.

Adult Birds

The terms 'hardbill' and 'softbill' are somewhat old-fashioned, but are useful as a quick guide for feeding common garden birds. It should be remembered that many species of hardbills feed their young on insects, and most types of adult garden bird will take some seeds, fruit and insects. The term 'hardbill' refers to seed-eating birds, and the term 'softbill' refers to those birds that require other types of food. It is important to identify the type of bird you have and the type of food that it eats in the wild. Examples of birds and the foods they can be fed on

Notice how the inner eyelid closes, as if with pleasure, as the bird is fed.

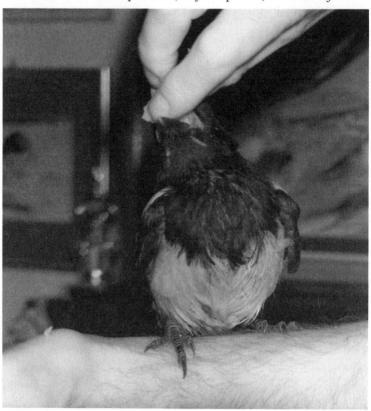

are given below. As far as possible, birds should be offered a staple diet supplemented with a variety of additional foods.

hardbills	*softbills*
(feed mainly on seeds)	*(feed mainly on insects)*
bullfinch	blackbird
goldfinch	starling
greenfinch	song thrush
hawfinch	mistle thrush
chaffinch	blue tit
feral pigeon	great tit
wood pigeon	long tailed tit
collared dove	house martin
turtle dove	swift
stock dove	nightingale
redpoll	wren
linnet	robin
waxwing	pied wagtail

house sparrow
tree sparrow
hedge sparrow

It is a common mistake to feed sparrows only on seed — they also need some insect food.

Most birds arrive in poor condition and they may not recognize a feeding dish as a source of food. Therefore it is often best to start them off on something they like. Most garden birds like raw mince meat and/or biscuits.

Pigeons, doves and finches

Hardbills can be fed on proprietary pet shop food for budgies, doves, etc. *Grit must always be available.* Never give birds seed without also giving them grit. Lime is needed by pigeons and bits of oyster shells or mineralized grit can be offered. Pigeons

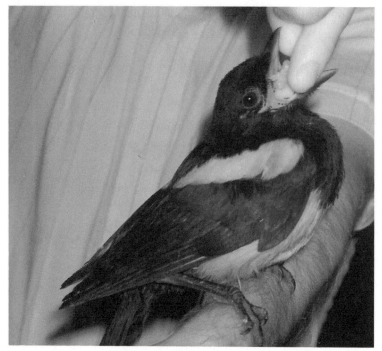

It is usually easy to feed magpies.

can also be offered peas, beans and rice. Pigeons are particularly fond of hemp, and this should be given as an extra and
not as part of their main diet as they will eat it to the exclusion
of everything else. Pigeons should be offered greens once or
twice a week.

Blackbirds, sparrows, thrushes, swifts and sparrows
Softbills such as tits, thrushes, swifts and house martins can be
fed on proprietary insect food bought from a pet shop. They
also enjoy raw mince, hard-boiled eggs and cat/dog food.

Adult swifts can be fed on a mixture of 75% mince meat
and 25% insect bird food moistened with water. Recipe 2 is
also suitable, and they will enjoy mealworms, with a pinch of
vitamin powder (SA37 is suitable). They need to be hand fed.

70

Song birds are fond of bacon rind and shredded suet. Sparrows will need a supply of seed and grit in addition to their insect food. They enjoy millet, and pet shop budgie food.

Crows, magpies, jays and coots

Birds such as crows, magpies and jays will eat a variety of food. They can be fed on poultry pellets, hard-boiled eggs, soaked puppy biscuits and bread. They are very fond of raw mince and tinned cat/dog food. Coots also need some pigeon corn and greens.

Birds of prey

Birds of prey can be fed on fresh, chopped cat/dog food such as heart. Mince is also useful for birds of prey, and they require some feathers/fur and bone. Rabbit legs, dead mice, one-day-old chicks and sterilized bonemeal are all suitable. Add a pinch of vitamin powder every other day if possible. As a rough guide, tawny owls will eat two to three dead day-old chicks daily with the addition of a mouse twice a week. Barn owls will sometimes only eat rodents. Vitamin supplements, dead mice and dead day-old chicks can usually be bought from large pet shops. If given an open aviary with rotting branches, most owls will scavenge for worms and beetles.

Birds of prey form pellets or castings which are regurgitated. This is normal.

Fish-eaters/seabirds

Fish-eaters such as grebes can be fed on fresh fish such as whitebait, sprats or sardines. Birds such as herons can eat 6 - 12 sprats a day and the fish should be offered wet and whole. Many fish-eaters have to be hand-fed whilst in captivity; when offering whole fish, give it to the bird head first as otherwise the gills may stick in the throat. Add ½ teaspoon of vitamin supplement every other day (obtainable from pet shops and veterinary surgeons). It is always wise to add a vitamin supplement when feeding birds largely on fish diets. Some birds enjoy fish dipped in cod liver oil once or twice a week. Gulls eat most of the foods that crows eat; in captivity sometimes they will only eat fish.

Some water birds may have difficulty in messing if they are not allowed on water, so give them a large bowl of water.

A large bucket of salt water (one dessertspoon salt to one pint water) should be offered to seabirds along with their normal drinking water. This is to keep their salt glands working.

Ducks, geese, swans and chickens

Ducks, geese, swans and chickens can be fed on chick crumbs, mash and pellets. They also like potatoes, cabbage, lettuce and grass. Greens should be offered daily. They will usually help themselves if left in a pen during the day. On farms ducks and chickens were often fed entirely on table scraps.

All birds like a varied diet. Seed can be soaked in cod liver oil once or twice a week. Most birds will enjoy biscuits, nuts, fruit (dried and fresh), berries and table scraps. Boiled potatoes and bread are eaten by a wide variety of birds, and so is shredded suet, raw mince, cheese and bacon rind. All birds should be offered some table scraps and some green foods. Chickweed and the seeding heads of grasses and dandelions are particularly enjoyed by smaller birds. Turnip greens, carrot tops, celery tops, lettuce and cabbage are all suitable. Peas, beans and rice are also enjoyed by many birds. Blackbirds and other birds such as thrushes, starlings and robins will enjoy mealworms. For tits, see also p. 65.

All adult birds must be given a source of water. However, some birds do not drink much. Birds of prey will usually obtain enough liquid from their food. Practically all birds will show some flexibility in feeding habits and adapt to captive feeding.

5 HOUSING, CLIPPING, HANDLING AND TRANSPORT

On arrival, spray/powder birds with a bird insecticide.

Birds have a higher body temperature than humans and they should feel warm. *Sick birds and baby birds must be kept in a heated environment, preferably at about 28°C.*

BABY BIRDS

Unfeathered baby birds can be kept in incubators, in hospital cages, on radiators, on heating pads, on hot-water/gel bottles, or under 60 watt table lights (avoiding the glare — ceramic lights are better). The temperature near the bird should be about 28°C. Do not allow a source of direct heat to come into contact with the bird's body. Whatever source of heat is used, the temperature around the bird should not be too hot, but just warm to the touch. It must be constant. Keeping a bird near a radiator which is turned off at night would not suffice. Heating pads are quite suitable if they can be left on day and night. A bird that is too hot may pant, stretch its neck, and show other signs of distress. A bird that is too cold will be cold to the touch, listless and will keep its head close to its body; it may shiver and fluff up its feathers.

If a bird gets too cold it may die. Therefore it is wise to keep it a little too warm rather than let it get cold.

Baby birds like to hide in a secure, darkened place and single naked birds can be wrapped in rags, old woollies, tissues or put into the cut-out toes of old socks. Bubble wrap (used for wrapping parcels) or foil are particularly useful as they retain the heat.

If you have more than one naked bird, put them into a small dish lined with some warm material so that they can keep each other warm, and put a loose cover on them. Absorbent tissue around the 'nest' is also useful as nestlings do not like to dirty their own 'nests', and at most feeding times they will deposit their droppings onto the tissue and not into their 'nests'.

Once the bird is fully feathered and standing, it will not require a heat source, provided the room is kept at 21°C day and night (normal room temperature). If you are unsure about the heating it would be wise to maintain a heat source until the bird is self-sufficient.

As the bird grows, it can be put into a plastic food container or a cardboard box. Line the box with newspaper and a layer of absorbent kitchen tissue.

Once the bird begins to fly, cover the box with net curtaining, or any transparent material. If the box is dark, the bird will not be able to learn to feed itself. Young birds that need force feeding, but have left the nest (fledglings) are usually terrified of being handled. Keep them in a large box with a small box inside where they can hide.

Once the bird is self-sufficient, it can be left in an unheated room for a few days to acclimatize before being transferred to an aviary. Alternatively, it could be let out in an aviary during the daytime and brought into an unheated room at night for a few days, before being left in the aviary during the day and night. The method you use obviously depends upon the housing available, the type of bird and the weather, especially as young birds will often sit in the rain and become chilled.

If the bird is alert and curious (as this one obviously is) and very much aware of its surroundings, then it is doing reasonably well.

Ducklings and chicks

Maintain the heat supply (at about 28°C) for about a week. Acclimatize them by leaving them at 21°C for three to four days and then transfer them to an unheated room for a further three to four days before transferring them to an aviary or closed pen.

Alternatively, let them out into a closed pen during the day-time and bring them into an unheated room at night for a few days, before leaving them in a closed pen or aviary during day and night.

Birds such as ducks should not be allowed onto water until they aretwo or threer months old, when they are preening themselves and using their oil glands. Therefore, do not leave an open bowl of water in their pens. Use a water feeder, or a saucer with a heavy upturned flowerpot in it so that the birds can drink, but cannot get into the water.

Once the birds are waterproof and are feeding well, they can be released at a suitable site (see pp. 83, 89).

Large birds can be housed for observation purposes in large temporary cages lined with newspaper. Sawdust and sand is useful for very messy patients, but hay and straw are best avoided because of the risk of infection.

ADULT BIRDS

Wherever possible, newly arrived birds should be isolated for a few days and checked for any signs of disease before putting them with other birds. Keep diseased birds isolated. Also isolate birds that look abnormal, as other birds may peck at ulcerated eyes, prolapses, etc.

Birds kept together must be examined for disease regularly. They should be treated with insecticide and wormed as necessary. Overcrowding leads to disease and fighting.

As with baby birds, sick adults need to be kept warm (28°C) day and night whilst they are poorly. And, as with baby birds, acclimatize them as above before letting them outside.

Never leave a sickly bird in an aviary at night.

It is best to avoid putting wild birds in cages because, if the bird can fly, it will fly at the wire in fright. Many birds break their necks this way. Birds the size of pigeons or bigger are usually safe in cages. Cardboard boxes lined with newspaper and absorbent tissue or sawdust are suitable. Open the top of the box and put net curtains or some other transparent material over the top. If a cage has to be used, use one that is boxed in on three sides or hang a cloth over it so that only the front is exposed. Do not leave a sickly bird or a young bird alone with other birds unless you are sure that it is all right. Birds may attack each other, even when the same species, when in a confined space. Remember also that crows will eat pigeons, birds of prey may attack crows, and magpies will eat quite large fledglings such as mistle thrush. Coots are predators, and, although they eat insects, eggs, mice and fish, they will also take chicks and other small birds. Consequently, caution is necessary when deciding to house different species of birds together. Even housing predator birds separate but within sight of potential prey can be extremely distressing for the birds. Timid birds may upset the more settled aviary residents.It is illegal to keep a bird in a container in which it cannot stretch its wings.

Birds that cannot fly must have a sheltered area; you should provide slanting perches so that they can climb up them to roost. Most birds like to sleep off the ground and a sickly bird which is left to sleep on grass or earth will usually die.

Most birds like to bathe.

Pigeons and birds of prey are happy in a shed; but it should have a window. Converted sheds are sometimes preferable to aviaries for recuperating wild birds because there is no netting for them to fly at. For long-term and resident birds, an aviary is usually best. Leave no gaps in the aviary where a cat could put its paw through. Also, note that cats and foxes will become diligent diggers when they see a potential meal. Buried wire may not suffice, even when the base is bent outwards, and a two-foot sunken wooden or brick base around the aviary may be necessary. Remember that some wood preservers are toxic to birds. Ledges are necessary for the comfort of birds of prey and birds such as pigeons. A variety of ledges and perches should be supplied and birds such as magpies like to make themselves little dens. They can also get bored and should be given some old pieces of wood to play with. Also supply birds with a little place where they can hide away when you enter the aviary to feed them, and of course an enclosed area to roost.

Birds that are usually penned, such as swans and geese, should be kept in closed pens at night, especially in areas where there are foxes.

Always keep bird rooms and aviaries well ventilated and avoid staying in such places for long periods of time. This is to prevent the development of allergies and to prevent catching any diseases from birds. Clean and disinfect bird houses regularly and treat them for parasites such as mites.

Some birds that cannot be released make very good pets, but potentially dangerous birds should never be trusted. Even a tame parrot can give you an extremely painful bite if you happen to hurt it! *Never leave a wild bird as big as a magpie alone in a room with a baby, and, in general, sick birds should be kept well away from babies and young children.*

Wing clipping

Adult wild birds should not be pinioned (an irreversible technique where a small piece of bone is removed from the wing tip, preventing the primary flight feathers from growing, and the bird from flying). It should anyway only be done by a vet. Wild birds should only be pinioned in exceptional circumstances, whilst young. Wing clipping might be justified if the bird needs to be grounded due to illness. A quill haemorrhage might occur if a wing is badly clipped. A better method is to strip the flight feathers of one wing. This is done by removing the vanes of each feather, leaving the shaft. The feathers will be replaced.

If the main flight feathers of both wings are clipped (cut right across, using a pair of sharp scissors or toe clippers) birds can sometimes remain balanced and fly on their secondaries. Preferably get your vet to do this. Clipping one wing would upset their balance enough to prevent escape, but without rendering the bird totally helpless against cats and other predators. The flight feathers will regrow at the annual moult when reclipping will have to be carried out. Clipping should be done across the main flights, but well away from the fleshy end of the wing or any partially grown feathers that are still forming (blood quills). Cutting incorrectly may result in injury or infection and should be caried out by an experienced person. Again, it is strongly recommended that stripping the flight feathers of one wing be carried out in preference to clipping.

Beak and toe clipping

You can buy specially shaped scissors for beak and toe clipping. Wild birds should not normally need such clipping, but

Hold a bird firmly, not too tightly. This magpie was completely blind in one eyes.

it may be necessary following an illness. Hold the bird under a light to see where the blood supply ends. Avoid clipping near to the blood supply.

Transport

Birds will put up with long-distance transport and a great deal of noise with no adverse effects. A baby bird can be put into a box and taken on shopping trips when necessary. Use a small box so that the bird cannot move around much and hurt itself. The box can be packed with newspaper and tissue to make a nest.

Unfeathered and partially feathered baby birds should not be transported without a source of heat. A hot-water bottle or a brandy bottle/shampoo bottle filled with warm water can be used. Wrap the bird in rags or the cut-out toes of old socks.

Large birds such as swans can be transported by wrapping

them in a towel and then putting them in a large laundry bag.

Handling

Small birds can be crushed by inexperienced handlers. Hold the bird just tight enough to prevent escape. Small birds can be restrained by holding their heads between the first and second fingers, so that undue pressure is not exerted on the body.

When handling birds with strong beaks and talons, it is advisable to wear gloves and glasses or a protective mask. Even when feeding birds of prey and birds such as herons, it is advisable to wear gloves and glasses. Birds of prey are not the only birds to have strong claws. The toes of crows can scratch, and

To avoid squeezing a bird, an inexperienced handler can hold a small bird with the head between the first two fingers. The bird is restrained without exerting pressure on the bird.

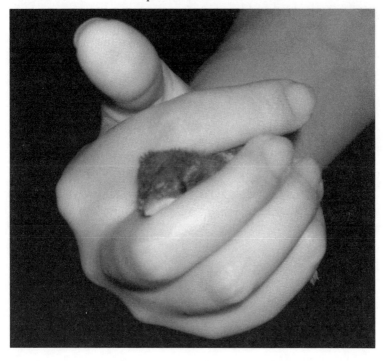

coots have long toe claws which can be extremely sharp. Even tiny swift claws will painfully cling to flesh.

Immobilize the wings of swans, geese and ducks by grabbing these first.

Avoid chasing birds. Use a net or throw a sheet over them if you can, or corner them and shoo them into a box. The clever way of catching birds, if you can manage it, is to lay a cardboard box on its side and prop up the lid with a stick, attached to a long piece of string. In the box place some food. When the bird goes in to get the food, pull the string, and, hey presto, your bird is in the box.

Birds can be caught most easily at night, when they are sleeping. Their feet lock onto their perch when asleep, so extra care is necessary to ease their feet gently off the perch.

When treating a bird, a cloth over the head will help to pacify it. If a bird suddenly starts to pant whilst you are holding it, immediately pop it into a dark box for about 15 minutes.

6 RELEASING

The aim of taking in a wild bird should, firstly, be to prevent unnecessary suffering and, secondly, to rehabilitate if possible.

Wild birds are at first tame and trusting. Once they become self-sufficient they should become shy and defensive. Once the bird has become defensive, after a couple of weeks in an aviary, it should be ready for release (except in the case of crows, which are kept until September). Beware of getting too close to wild birds, as this may make them more difficult to rehabilitate.

Many thousands of wild birds die each year. They are vulnerable, particularly in their first year of life, to predation, starvation and cold. The birds you are likely to find in trouble are generally the weakest ones, perhaps with bad eyesight, etc. All you can hope to achieve is to give the bird a second chance — a second bite at the apple. Once you have a wild bird, it is your duty to prevent undue suffering. If, for instance, a bird has a wing injury and cannot fly, and you release it, then the bird will inevitably suffer. It would be more humane to ask your vet to destroy it if you cannot nurse it or find anyone else to nurse it.

Captive wild birds

If a bird cannot be released for any reason then you must decide whether or not it can have a reasonable existence in captivity. Remember that if a bird needs to be kept in captivity it may live for over ten years. Wood pigeons and herring gulls, for instance, are capable of living for twenty years in captivity, although their average life spans in the wild are about two and three years respectively.

Birds usually respond better when there are a few other birds around (provided they are of the same/similar species and not too territorial).

Remember also that certain types of wild bird must be registered and ringed if kept in captivity and a list of such birds can be obtained from the Department of the Environment.

Bird ringing

Closed rings
Closed rings are suitable for very young nestlings. Choose the correct size ring for the type of bird. The foot must be small enough to have a ring fitted over it without too much effort, and large enough to stop it falling off again. It is always better to fit it early rather than leaving it too late. Hold the nestling in one hand and slip the ring over all the forward pointing toes. Slide the ring up the leg as far as it will go and gently ease out the backward pointing toe. Record the ring number with the other details of the bird, for example date of arrival, release, etc.

Split rings
Split metal rings and plastic rings can be put on birds of any age and are useful for identification. Again, care is necessary when choosing the correct ring size for the type of bird. Never put two rings on the same foot.

British Trust for Ornithology rings
The British Trust for Ornithology may have a member in your

area who would be willing to ring a rare bird for you prior to release They may then receive information about the bird if it is found later.

Bird rings can be bought, but it is usually assumed that they are for show birds. You need to be absolutely sure that the size is correct for the type of bird you wish to ring. The groups of birds listed are just a guide, and it is always best to check with the suppliers. The size letters may differ with different suppliers. The Department of the Environment will supply rings for rare birds which must be registered and ringed.

closed rings	examples of types of birds	plastic split rings
A	wren, chiffchaff (red-eared waxbills)	XF
B	coal tit, siskin, twite, long tailed tit	
	(cordon bleu)	XF
C	blue tit, linnet (hecks)	XF
D	chaffinch, goldfinch, bullfinch	
	(zebra finch)	XF
E	house sparrow, hedge sparrow, green-	
	finch (Bengalese finch)	XCS
G	great tit, skylark	
	(border and roller canaries)	XCL
J	lesser woodpecker, corn bunting	
	(crested canaries)	XCL
K	hawfinch, waxwing	
	(Java sparrow)	XB
L	starling, song thrush	
	(budgerigar)	XB
M	mistle thrush, blackbird	
	(lovebirds)	X3
P	jay (cockatiels)	1FB
R	jackdaw, magpie, dove	
	(tumbler pigeons)	1FB

S	little owl (homing pigeons)	2FB
U	barn owl, tawny owl,	(for larger birds
	short-eared owl	special rings and
		clips are available)

Names in brackets are the show/pet birds for which the rings are usually supplied.

A TIME TO RELEASE

In general, once a bird is fully recovered and self-sufficient, it can be released after a couple of weeks in an aviary. If you don't have an aviary, let the bird exercise in a garage or shed (if it has windows). Put nets over windows to prevent birds flying into them. The same applies to baby birds. Once they are feeding themselves they can be released after a couple of weeks in an aviary. Avoid keeping wild birds longer than is necessary, and never release them directly from a window of a heated room. They will surely die unless they have become acclimatized to the outside temperature first.

Avoid releasing birds in bitter winter conditions, when it is windy or when it is raining. Preferably release in the spring and summer months, when the weather is mild, and when there is a forecast of three days of reasonably good weather. Let them go in the morning, after feeding them, except in the case of nocturnal birds, which should be released in the evening.

Starvation is one of the main factors controlling bird populations. Therefore, to give a bird the best possible chance of rehabilitation, especially if it has been hand-reared, release it when there is plenty of food available. In January–March the food supply for birds is generally at its lowest, and individuals must compete for the food available. Many young and weak birds will starve at this time of year. This applies especially to hardbills which rely on grain supplies. Unless the ground is hard, frozen or covered in snow, diligent softbills, which rely on a supply of insects, may be able to find enough food to survive. It is preferable to release softbills after wet weather, when the ground is soft. If there is a summer drought and the ground is very hard, then insect-eating birds may have a difficult time finding food.

A place to release

Many people believe that adult birds should be released where they were found. This is recommended when a bird has been kept for a relatively short time and may have a mate waiting for it. However, in many cases this is impractical. Birds are often found in unsuitable or inconvenient places, and where you cannot return daily to see if they need feeding.

It is not always suitable to release birds into an area where there are many birds of the same species. A new bird intruding into another bird's territory may be evicted by the resident bird — or even attacked. On the other hand, some birds flock, and need to be near others of the same species. Some flock at certain times of year. However, if you release a bird in an area where there are no other birds of the same species, the absence of birds may be indicative of the absence of suitable food, and the bird may die. In general, after releasing a bird, always ensure that it has a supply of food and water available daily until it is no longer required.

RELEASING SPECIFIC BIRDS

Birds of prey

Hand-reared birds of prey need to be released slowly. Owls are usually easy to release. They can be released in the same way as garden birds — from an aviary — but be prepared to feed them daily for several months whilst they are learning to find food.

You need a licence to release barn owls, so contact the Department of the Environment if you are planning to release one.

Basically the same method of release applies to juvenile raptors, but the timing is very important. The releasing process needs to begin as soon as they are ready to leave the nest. They can be transferred to a nest box which has been made from cutting a large hole in a plastic canister, or by using a tea chest or barrel which is open at one end: about 60 cm x 60 cm x 60 cm is usually an adequate opening size. Half board the opening to prevent them from falling out. The nest can be put in an open aviary or positioned at the release site. Again the birds might continue to need feeding for many months. The aviary technique is suitable for kestrels. For the larger birds of prey it would be wise to seek specialist advice on the species concerned.

It is often difficult to successfully release older birds of prey which have missed the releasing process when they are just ready to leave the nest.

Some types of adult bird that have been taken into care because of injuries can be released from an aviary. Sometimes they will also return to feed for a few days. Owls, kestrels and sparrowhawks can be treated in this way, but again, for the larger birds of prey it would be wise to seek specialist advice on the species concerned. Some birds of prey are very timid and need to be kept in sheds.

Crows, magpies and jays
Baby crows and other members of the corvidae family should preferably be about three months old and fully grown before release so that they can fend for themselves, and stand up to the bullying of other members of the corvidae family. Release young birds in August/September if possible.

Ducks and game

Ducks may stay around, especially if they are getting free breakfast and dinner. If you nurse game, then it would be sensible to avoid releasing them during the shooting season.

Garden birds

In many cases garden birds can be released from an aviary into the garden. Hand-reared garden birds can be left in an aviary for a couple of weeks before releasing them. They should then be familiar with their surroundings and this will help them in their quest for food. Once the birds have been released, leave food out in the garden for them. Leave the food daily until the birds do not return to feed. Sometimes birds will return to feed, in adverse weather conditions, a long time after their release. Sometimes released birds want to return to the aviary. They can be locked in at night and released again in the morning.

Pet birds

Escaped pet birds are often found. They can be treated the same as wild birds, but they should not be released.

Birds such as budgies may be attacked by sparrows, and barbary doves are not very good at avoiding cats. Some parrots have been known to form colonies in the south of England, but they usually die if the winter is particularly bad.

You may be able to find the original owner or a new home for an escaped pet bird by advertising locally.

Pigeons

Feral pigeons are stayers and they can be released into a suitable open space, where they can find food and where you can keep an eye on them. If you release them from your patch they may stay there for ever more, especially if they are getting free breakfast and dinner.

On the other hand, wood pigeons will take off like jets and

you will probably never see them again. It is best to release wood pigeons as soon as possible, even if the weather is not ideal, as they are very timid and will fly at the aviary wire when you approach the aviary. It is only a matter of time before one breaks its neck.

Racing pigeons

Racing pigeons need to be kept for about six months and then they can be released. Carry them out of the aviary and release them a short distance away just before feeding time. They will then return to the aviary for food. They can then be gradually released along with other pigeons.

Swans

A swan known to have a territory and a mate should be released back to its territory, but check first that another bird has not taken its territory and mate. At the beginning and end of the year territorial behaviour is strong and due consideration must be given to the possibility of territorial conflicts. It is usually best to release juvenile swans into non-breeding flocks. They can then integrate into the social group.

Swifts

Put a ramp at an angle of 45° in the juvenile bird's container. When the bird is preparing to leave it will try to climb the ramp. Take the bird out and let it hang from your gloved hand. It if is ready to leave, it will let go and fly away. Put a cushion on the ground, or do it over grass, in case it drops off. If it is not ready, try again the next day. Release adult swifts as soon as possible because if they do not use their wings for a long time the muscles will degenerate and they will be unable to fly; though this should not happen over one winter. Adult swifts should also be released from the hand. Or they can be thrown gently into the air so that they can catch the air currents and be off. Again, always do this over grass.

Swallows and martins

As with swifts, these birds feed on the wing and therefore have to be hand-fed whilst in captivity. They can be released from an aviary.

Remember to wash your hands after handling wild birds and never kiss them.

USEFUL PRODUCTS, NAMES AND ADDRESSES

antiseptic	useful for cuts and bites:from pet shops
canker treatment*	from pet supply stores; advertised in *Cage and Aviary Birds*; from John Haith, Park Street, Cleethorpes, South Humberside DN35 7NF
coccidiosis treatment	from pet shops; advertised in *Cage and Aviary Birds*
dead chicks and mice	from pet shops; advertised in *Cage and Aviary Birds*
Dermisol cream	very useful for cuts; sold by veterinary practices
heating pads/hospital cages/lamps	rom pet supply stores; advertised in *Cage and Aviary Birds*
Hills Feline Maintenance Science Diet	sold by veterinary practices and some pet shops
insect food	from pet supply stores and some pet shops; advertised in *Cage and Aviary Birds*
insecticide bird spray/powder/cream	from pet supply stores; advertised in *Cage and Aviary Birds* and also some pet shops
Kaosal/Kaogel	useful for poisoning; sold by veterinary practices
micropore tape/zinc oxide tape	medical dressing tape useful for broken bones; from chemists

rearing food**	from pet supply stores;advertised in *Cage and Aviary Birds*; some pet shops
Swarfega	hand-cleansing gel: useful for cleaning greasy birds; from builders' merchants
vitamin powder (e.g. SA37)	from pet supply stores; advertised in *Cage and AviaryBirds;* also some pet shops
worm treatment*	from pet supply stores; advertised in *Cage and Aviary Birds;* also some pet shops

* Your local veterinary surgeon should also be able to help.

** Hand rearing foods should not be confused with the special foods available for *adult* breeding birds.

Addresses

British Bird Council
1577 Bristol Road South, Birmingham B45 9UA
tel 0121 453 9284

British Trust for Ornithology
The Nunnery, Thetford, Norfolk IP24 2PU
tel 01842 750050

Cage and Aviary Birds
PO Box 272, Haywards Heath, West Sussex RH16 3FS
tel 01444 441212

Department of the Environment — Wildlife Division, Birds Branch
Room 809, Tollgate House, Houlton Street, Bristol BS2 9DJ
tel 0117 878000

International Ornithological Association
62 Northwood Drive, Sittingbourne, Kent ME10 4QS
tel 01795 425940

First Aid for Wild Birds

International Union for the Conservation of Nature
Rue Mauverney 28, CH-1196 Gland, Switzerland

Ministry of Agriculture, Fisheries and Food (MAFF)
Whitehall Place, London SW1A 2HH
tel 0171 273 3000
poisoning hotline 0800 321600

Royal Pigeon Racing Association
Reddings House, The Reddings, Nr Cheltenham, Glos GL51 6RN
tel 01452 713529

RSNC Wildlife Trusts Partnership
The Green, Witham Park, Waterside South, Lincoln LN5 7JR
tel 01522 544400

RSPCA
Causeway, Horsham, West Sussex RH12 1HG
tel 01403 64181

RSPB (Royal Society for Protection of Birds)
The Lodge, Sandy, Bedfordshire SG19 2BL
tel 01767 680551

Wildlife Hospital Trust
Aston Road, Haddenham, Buckinghamshire HP17 8AF
tel 01844 292292

INDEX